LAKE SUPERIOR

A TRUE BOOK

by

Ann Armbruster

Children's Press®

A Division of Grolier Publishing

New York London Hong Kong Sydney
Danbury, Connecticut

Reading Consultant
Linda Cornwell
*Learning Resource Consultant
Indiana Department of
Education*

Subject Consultant
William D. Ellis
*Editor of the quarterly journal
of the Great Lakes
Historical Society*

Winter on Lake Superior

Library of Congress Cataloging-in-Publication Data

Armbruster, Ann.
    Lake Superior / by Ann Armbruster.
       p.   cm. — (A true book)
    Includes index.
    Summary: Discusses the history, nautical stories, and industrial and
social significance of Lake Superior.
    ISBN 0-516-20015-1 (lib. bdg.)   ISBN 0-516-26106-1(pbk.)
    1. Superior, Lake—Juvenile literature. [1. Superior, Lake.] I. Title.
II. Series.
F552.A76 1996
977.4'9—dc20   96-2027
                                       CIP
                                       AC

Contents

The Largest Lake   5

Lac Supérieur   9

Sault Sainte Marie   11

The Soo Canals   14

Hiawatha   20

The *Edmund Fitzgerald*   24

Isle Royale   32

Natural Resources   36

Lake Superior Today   42

To Find Out More   44

Important Words   46

Index   47

Meet the Author   48

The Largest Lake

Lake Superior stretches across the border between the United States and Canada. It is one of the Great Lakes— five large lakes that lie in the heart of eastern North America. The other four lakes are Lake Erie, Lake Huron, Lake Michigan, and Lake Ontario.

C A N

O N T A R I O

Thunder
Bay ■

Minnesota

Isle
Royale

Duluth
■

LAKE SUPERIOR

Keweenaw
Peninsula

Whitefish
Bay

Sault Ste. Marie

Sault Ste.
Marie
■

Soo Canals

St. Marys River

M i c h i g a n

Wisconsin

LAKE MICHIGAN

LAKE HURON

LAKE ERIE

LAKE C

Illinois

Indiana

Ohio

Pennsylvan

U N I T E D   S T A

Lake Superior is the largest, deepest, and cleanest of the Great Lakes. It holds one-tenth of all the freshwater on Earth. And it covers 31,700 square miles (82,100 square kilometers).

In the United States, Lake Superior is bordered by Minnesota, Wisconsin, and Michigan. In Canada, it is bordered by the province of Ontario.

Lac Supérieur

Jean Nicolet, a French explorer, crossed the Atlantic Ocean to North America in 1618. He was seeking a water route to Asia. Instead, he found the natural wealth of North America—an inland ocean of freshwater.

Nicolet named this inland

Jean Nicolet came to North America in search of the Northwest Passage—a water route to Asia. Instead, he found Lake Superior.

sea *Lac Supérieur*, French for "Upper Lake." The name meant that Lake Superior was upstream from the other Great Lakes.

Sault Sainte Marie

At its eastern end, Lake Superior empties into Lake Huron through St. Marys River, creating dangerous rapids. The water level between Lake Superior and Lake Huron drops 20 feet (6 meters) over a chain of waterfalls.

When Europeans first came to the Great Lakes, the falls cut off

St. Marys rapids made it impossible for ships to pass.

navigation between Lake Superior and the lower lakes. Ships could not get through, so people settled near the falls for more than three hundred years. The French called the area *Sault Sainte Marie*, meaning the "Falls of St. Mary."

Two cities with the same name stand on opposite sides

Sault Ste. Marie, Michigan (top left), and Sault Ste. Marie, Ontario (top right), are connected by the International Bridge (bottom).

of the rapids—Sault Ste. Marie, Michigan, and Sault Ste. Marie, Ontario. They are connected by the famous International Bridge.

13

The Soo Canals

In the 1840s, Americans
developed iron and copper
mines on the south shore of
Lake Superior. In those days,
boats had to be hauled
around St. Marys Falls on
skids and rollers. Then the
cargo was transported on
land. All that loading and
unloading took weeks of hard

An 1850s ship passes through the Sault Ste. Marie Canals.

work. There had to be another way around the falls.

In 1855, the first canal was built. A wood-burning steamer made the trip from Lake Huron to Lake Superior. The upper and lower lakes were finally linked.

Today the Sault Ste. Marie Canals—known as the Soo Canals—are made up of two canals. One is operated by the United States, the other by Canada. Locks lower or

Soo Canal locks raise and lower ships when they enter Lake Huron or Lake Superior.

raise ships to the level of the lake they wish to enter.

The Soo Canal locks are among the busiest in the world. Iron ore, grain, coal, and oil are major products transported through the waterways. About 85 million tons (77 million metric tons) of cargo pass through the canals each year.

Two ports are the most active—Duluth and Thunder Bay. Duluth lies in Minnesota at the western end of Lake Superior. It is one of the

Cargo brought to Duluth then travels by railroad to its final destination (above). Thunder Bay has the largest grain elevators in the world (right).

United States's busiest inland seaports. Thunder Bay, in Ontario, Canada, is the center of that country's paper industry. Thunder Bay also has the largest grain elevators in the world.

A freighter leaves
the Soo Canals.

The Soo Canals benefit
both the United States and
Canada. They are very important to the economy of the
entire Great Lakes and St.
Lawrence River region.

Hiawatha

Lake Superior is not only important to the region, but it is mentioned in literature as well. In 1855, an American poet named Henry Wadsworth Longfellow published *The Song of Hiawatha*. The hero of this book-length poem is Hiawatha, a young

The illustration above for *The Song of Hiawatha*, written by Henry Wadsworth Longfellow (inset), shows Hiawatha and a friend scanning the landscape.

American Indian who lives along the shores of Lake Superior. Longfellow got the hero's name from a book of Indian legends.

Longfellow's Hiawatha could take mile-long steps and out-run an arrow. He lived in the land of Gitchee Gumee, and he married Minnehaha. The poem became very popular. Many people read about swift-footed Hiawatha running along the deep, cold lake.

There was a real Hiawatha. His name was Manabozho. He was a Mohawk Indian, who founded the Five Nations of the Iroquois League.

Some people say Manabozho
was a great peacemaker who
formed laws for the Iroquois to
live as one people. Some histori-
ans do not agree. Others say that
some of those laws found their
way into the U.S. Constitution.

The Edmund Fitzgerald

Lake Superior has even more exciting stories—such as the one about the *Edmund Fitzgerald*, a 726-foot (221-m) supership. The ship, nick-named *Big Fitz*, left Duluth early on November 10, 1975. It was bound for the Soo Canals.

That day, a fierce winter storm struck Lake Superior.

Big Fitz was a supership.

Thirty-foot (9-m) waves pound-
ed the ship. Winds up to 96
miles (154 km) per hour
whipped the lake. *Big Fitz*
plowed on through the raging
waters with twenty-nine crew
members aboard.

Lake Superior storms have a dangerous reputation.

That afternoon, the captain of *Big Fitz* radioed: "The seas are tremendous, the worst I have ever seen." Later, other ships tried to contact *Big Fitz*. There was no response. The *Edmund Fitzgerald* had vanished.

The next morning, a large oil slick was spotted near the ship's last known position. A search team found one of *Big Fitz's* lifeboats nearby. No wreckage was found.

Finance
Pages 2D to 5D

Races
Page 4E

Weather
Showers
Details on Page 5A

The Detroit News

AMERICA'S LARGEST EVENING CIRCULATION

TUESDAY, NOVEMBER 11, 1975

15 CENTS

AR NO. 81

reighter sinks; crew of 29
s hunted in Lake Superior

By CHARLES THEISEN
and JAMES McCLEAR
News Staff Writers

A 729-foot Great Lakes freighter bound for Detroit sank in Lak̶ ̶ ̶ ̶ ̶ ̶ ̶ ̶ ̶with a crew of 29 men. The ̶ ̶ ̶ ̶ ̶ ̶ ̶ ̶ ̶ ̶ the crew appare̶ ̶ ̶ ̶ ̶ ̶ ̶ ̶ ̶nal.

With the brea̶ ̶ ̶ ̶ ̶ ̶ ̶ the hunt for sur̶ ̶ ̶ ̶ ̶ ̶

The steame̶ ̶ ̶ ̶ ̶ heard from ̶ ̶ ̶ ̶ ̶ ̶ miles northwe̶ ̶ ̶ ̶ ̶ by hurricane-̶ ̶ ̶ ̶ ̶ one of the de̶ ̶ ̶ ̶ ̶ Capt. Jess̶ ̶ ̶ ̶ M. Anderson̶ ̶ ̶ ̶ ̶ distance of 10 ̶ ̶ ̶ ̶ a shore-to-ship telephone call early today ̶ ̶ ̶ the Fitzgerald "suddenly vanished from my radar screen."

The Anderson remained in the vicinity and radioed for help.

A small amount of debris — orange planking ̶ ̶ ̶ ̶ ̶ ̶ ̶ ̶ ̶believed to be from ̶ ̶ ̶

and the Coast Guard said there was no doubt the Fitzgerald sank.

There was no immediate sign of either survivors or bodies of victims.

The sinking of the Fitzgerald was the first Great Lakes shipping disaster in nine years. On Nov. 30, 1966, the freighter D.J. Morrell sank in ̶ ̶ ̶ ̶ ̶ the freighter ̶ ̶ 28 men.

feared by sailors for the savage winds waves accompanying the change of sea Most storm deaths and ship losses on the Lakes have occurred during November.

Two Coast Guard helicopters and an ai̶ flew immediately to the scene last night ever, the search was hampered not o̶ darkness but also by winds gusting to 5̶ an hour and waves as high as 20 feet. ̶ ̶ ̶ ̶ ̶ ̶ ̶ ̶ ̶ ̶utters Woodrush ̶ ̶ ̶ ̶ ̶ ̶rom Sault Ste ̶ ̶ ̶ ̶ ̶ea to search fe ̶ ̶ ̶ ̶ ̶was 400 miles ̶ ̶ ̶ ̶ ̶from the scene ̶ ̶ ̶ ̶ ruptured fuel ̶ ̶ ̶ ̶began to get u̶ ̶ ̶ ̶ ̶ending repairs. ̶ ̶ ̶ ̶d with the comi̶ ̶ ̶ ̶ ̶ters — the Rog̶ ̶ rt Henry – w̶ ̶ ̶ and arrived in ̶

̶ ̶ ̶ ̶ ̶joined the A̶ ̶ criss-crossing ̶ ̶ ̶area. The Canadia̶ sent two C130 aircraft to assist. But̶ rough seas and high winds preve̶ rapid response.
The William Clay Ford, upbound̶ without cargo, had passed the sce̶

Ship vanished from radar here

MICHIGAN

Concluded on Page 12A

A newspaper reports the news of the *Edmund Fitzgerald's* disappearance.

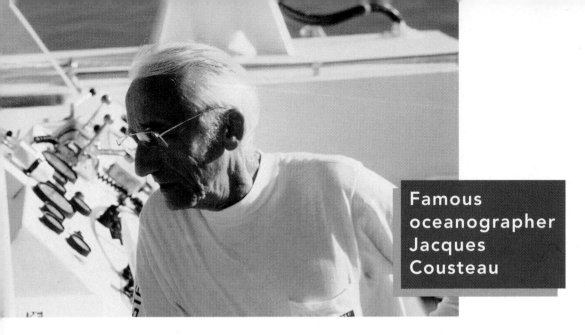

Famous oceanographer Jacques Cousteau

In 1980, underseas explorer Jacques Cousteau searched for the *Edmund Fitzgerald*. His famous ship *Calypso* located the wreckage at the bottom of Lake Superior. Because of icy water, divers could stay underwater for only a few minutes.

In the mid-1980s, the wreck of the *Edmund Fitzgerald* was investigated again. This time, computer-guided robots with cameras were lowered into the depths of Lake Superior. These robots could stay underwater for hours.

Experts studied the collected data. They said that *Big Fitz* had made a sharp plunge to the bottom of the lake, taking all its crew members with it.

Many ships and many sailors have been lost on the Great Lakes. But the mysterious disappearance of *Big Fitz* has become a symbol for all shipwrecks.

Whitefish Bay

The *Edmund Fitzgerald* sank in Whitefish Bay on Lake Superior. Whitefish Bay is on the lake's eastern end, near Sault Ste. Marie, Michigan and Ontario. The life preservers were among the few remains of the *Edmund Fitzgerald* the day after the tragedy.

Whitefish Bay is known as a graveyard for ships. It is thought that there are about sixty ships on the bottom of the bay. So many ships have met their end here that the Great Lakes Shipwreck Museum stands on its shores.

Isle Royale

Isle Royale, the largest island in Lake Superior, is almost all wilderness. Cars are not allowed on the island. The only transportation to the island is by seaplane or boat.

In 1931, Isle Royale was declared a national park. The park covers 570,000 acres (230,700 hectares) of wilder-

Isle Royale is covered with forests (above).
Canoes and kayaks (inset) can be used on
the lakes and streams of the island.

ness. Visitors may see beavers, muskrats, minks, and red foxes. They will also see gray wolves and the nation's largest herd of moose.

Recently, naturalists have used the island to study the relationship between wolves

(Counter clockwise from top) Moose, red foxes, gray wolves, minks, and beavers are all found on Isle Royale.

and moose. In this isolated wilderness laboratory, they can observe the animals in their own world.

The remains of ancient Indian copper mines have been found around the island. Thousands of years ago, the Old Copper Indians in the area made knives, fish-hooks, and harpoons from copper. They were among the first metalworkers of the world.

Natural Resources

In the mid-1800s, European explorers found the remains of other copper diggings in the region. Copper mines were established. The Keweenaw Peninsula on Lake Superior's south shore became a big source for copper. Michigan's Upper Peninsula became known as "copper

Copper mines were started up in the mid-1800s (above). This 6,000-pound (2,722-kg) piece of copper (right) was taken from an ancient mine. It has hammer marks of early prospectors.

country." The opening of the Soo Canals brought a great copper rush.

Copper

People mining copper in the 1800s found new uses for this metal. Copper was used in the development of the electric generator, which created electricity. It was also important for such inventions as Samuel F. B. Morse's telegraph in 1840, and Thomas Edison's lightbulb in 1879. Today in the United States, over half of the copper used is for the production of electricity.

Then in 1841, iron ore was discovered around Lake Superior. More prospectors flooded the area. But iron mining was dangerous. Many men were killed in the deep shafts of iron mines.

Gradually, modern mining methods were developed. Engines replaced horses. Electric lights replaced candles. Dynamite replaced gunpowder. Eventually, iron ore became a major export of the Great Lakes region.

Loggers
transport
logs down
a river.

Loggers arrived in the area, too. They cut oak, ash, dogwood, and other broad-leaf trees around Lake Superior.

One area was named the North Woods. These woods were full of pine trees—some more than one hundred years old. Their strong wood made

Early loggers used horses to move logs (above). Today, modern equipment is used (left).

the pines the most popular tree in the timber industry.

Over the years, logging ruined the North Woods. Today, that destructive time in history is known as the Big Cut.

Lake Superior Today

Much of the landscape around Lake Superior remains unchanged. Along the coastline, the rugged wilderness exists unspoiled.

Boating is popular on Lake Superior, and people fish for lake trout, bass, and walleyes. Hikers can walk for miles in the

Lake Superior provides outstanding views and recreation.

wilderness. Nature lovers can enjoy the spectacular scenery.

Today the area's natural resources are protected. People know the environment is fragile. They work together to preserve the health and beauty of Lake Superior, the largest Great Lake.

To Find Out More

Here are more places where you can explore Lake Superior and states and provinces around it:

 **Books**

 **Organizations**

Aylesworth, Thomas G., and Virginia L. Aylesworth. **State Reports: Western Great Lakes**. Chelsea House Publishers, 1991.

Fradin, Dennis Brindell. **Hiawatha, Messenger of Peace.** Macmillan Publishing, 1992.

MacKay, Kathryn. **Ontario.** Children's Press, 1992.

Porter, A. P. **Minnesota.** Lerner Publications, 1992.

Great Lakes Commission
400 Fourth St.
ARGUS II Bldg.
Ann Arbor, MI 48103-4816
(313) 665-9135
glc@glc.org

Michigan Travel Bureau
P.O. Box 30226
Lansing, MI 48909
1-800-5432-YES

Ontario Travel
Queens Park
Toronto, Ontario
Canada M7A 2E5
1-800-ONTARIO

Online Sites

Tour Lake Superior

http://www.great-lakes. net:2200/places/watsheds/ superior/superior.html

Discover the endless attractions of the Great Lakes Circle Tour. This online site has facts about Lake Superior, including information about conservation efforts around the lake.

Visit Minnesota

http://www.great-lakes.net: 2200/partners/GLC/pub/ circle/minn.html

Take the scenic North Shore Drive along Lake Superior. Visit the port of Duluth, Split Rock Lighthouse, Grand Portage National Monument, Voyageurs National Park, and more.

Explore Michigan

http://www.great-lakes.net: 2200/partners/GLC/pub/ circle/michigan.html

Wonders can be found in Michigan and the Great Lakes surrounding it. Visit the Upper Peninsula's white sand beaches, ghost towns, forts, and fishing villages, and enjoy Isle Royale National Park.

Facts and figures about the Great Lakes

http://www.great-lakes. net:2200/refdesk/almanac/ almanac.html

Includes information about populations and the region.

Important Words

canal man-made waterway for boats

cargo goods that a ship carries from one place to another

lock boxlike space that raises or lowers ships as they travel from one water level to another

navigation steering a boat through water

ore mineral that holds a valuable substance

prospector person who searches for minerals

rapids water flowing very fast over rocks

skids support, such as a log, used to raise something off the ground

Index

(**Boldface** page numbers
indicate illustrations.)

American Indians, 21–23, 35
beavers, 33, **34**
*Big Fitz. See Edmund
Fitzgerald*
Calypso, 28
Canada, 5, 8, 16, 19
copper, 14, 35, 36–37, **37**, 38
Cousteau, Jacques, 28, **28**
Duluth, Minnesota, 17–18,
18, 24
Edmund Fitzgerald, 24–29,
25, **27**, 30
grain elevators, 18, **18**
Great Lakes, 5–8, 10, 11,
19, 39
Great Lakes Shipwreck
Museum, 31
Hiawatha, 20–22, **21**, **23**
International Bridge, 13, **13**
iron mines, 14, 39
Iroquois Indians, 22–23
Isle Royale, 32–35, **33**
Keweenaw Peninsula, 36
Lake Huron, 11, 15
locks, 16–17, **16**
logging, 40–41, **40**, **41**
Longfellow, Henry
Wadsworth, 20–21, **21**

Manabozho, 22–23
minks, 33, **34**
Mohawk Indians, 22
moose, 33–35, **34**
muskrats, 33
Nicolet, Jean, 9, **10**
North America, 5, 9, **10**
North Woods, 40–41
Old Copper Indians, 35
ports, 18
railroads, **18**
red foxes, 33, **34**
St. Lawrence River, 19
St. Marys River, 11, **12**, 14
Sault Ste. Marie Canals, **15**,
16–17, **16**, 19, **19**, 24, 37
Sault Ste. Marie, Michigan,
13, **13**
Sault Ste. Marie, Ontario,
13, **13**
ships, 12, **15**, **16**, **19**,
24–29, **25**, 30–31, **31**
Soo Canals. *See* Sault Ste.
Marie Canals
storms, 24–26, **26**
Thunder Bay, Ontario,
17–18, **18**
United States, 5, 8, 16, 18,
19, 23
Whitefish Bay, 30–31
wolves, 33–35, **34**

Meet the Author

Living in Ohio, close to the Great Lakes, Ann Armbruster pursues her interest in history. A former English teacher and school librarian, she is the author of many books for children.